May.15.18

NETWORKING ON ÜBER STEROIDS

HOW TO MASTER A MORE POWERFUL WAY TO NETWORK

BrandON MILTSCH

Bartley,
So Excited to Meet You!

Let Me Know How I can
Help You.

#BrandoN

Printed in the United States of America

Second Printing, 2017

ISBN 978-1539967927

Networking on Uber Steroids
6199 N Federal Highway,
Boca Raton, FL 33487

www.NetworkingOnUberSteroids.com

NETWORKING ON ÜBER STEROIDS

BrandON Miltsch

WHO IS BrandON?

With drive, determination and a natural gift to create connections that grow businesses in a digital era, BrandON
Miltsch has made influential connections at the global
level. He understands sales, and he understands what's
needed to be successful with today's digital focus.
BrandON's rare ability to demystify technology helps his
clients harness the power of the Internet to ignite new
opportunities and grow their business.

With a solid track record of successful sales at Fortune
Global 500 Companies - along with over 10 years of
digital agency experience – BrandON brings together a
strong mix of expertise in social, marketing and business
development.

A genuine desire to make a meaningful contribution with
his life's work inspires BrandON to give back to the community. He has helped raise millions for the Frank Ski Kids
Foundation and other Atlanta organizations. Miltsch's
annual holiday party for Atlanta's business leaders,
celebrities and opinion elite delivered thousands of toys
to needy children throughout Atlanta every year.

PREFACE

School, books and tests were never my forte. They were too ordinary and too structured for my ambitions. Like so many other classmates, I found it difficult to focus on the mundane subjects at hand. I was defined as having a learning deficit. Those were very harsh words that reverberated negatively to me. Far worse, some "teachers" said I would never amount to much if I didn't take school more seriously. Really?

The truth of the matter was that, well, I was far too eager to experience the real world. I had true passion, ambition and enthusiasm to challenge status quo. I did have focus - it was singular and it was relentless in my drive for success on a grand scale. I knew I could be the best at whatever I wanted to do and become. I just didn't want to do it slowly, and I didn't want to do it on a small scale. It had to be big, and it had to have impact to the whole world.

2

It all started when I saw my father at only 37 years old reach his ambitions. His ad agency created extremely successful campaigns for blue chip clients. I admired the creative work he brought home to share with us, which included memorable ads for Bausch & Lomb, Exxon, GM, Kodak, and Xerox. This was far away from his humble beginnings as a young child growing up in Belgium. He was able to craft an ordinary life into an extraordinary one as both a father and successful businessman. My mother was also born of humble roots, rising up to become an admired and well-respected RN despite struggles that tested her resilience and fortitude. As a Labor and Delivery nurse, she loves to tackle the toughest of cases because that's where she feels the most reward.

With two great role models, I bet you are wondering why I chose the business world instead of medicine, that's simple - blood. Besides, there was something magical about my father's work. His work fueled my ambitions. When he became a CMO and worked at Fortune 50 global giants like NEC and NTT, his world became a lens to the future. I remember him telling me about "computer glasses" that were in an NEC lab in

Japan. That was 1997. I knew I wanted to be a part of that world - the world of the future.

After moving from Rochester, New York to West Palm Beach, Florida where I attended North-wood University, I became an official part of that world when I started working at NTT/Verio. It was a learning experience that allowed me to see more of the future and better understand the business world. I quickly became immersed in technology and found it my gateway to my future. There were bumps along the way. Actually, more like boulders. But I never doubted myself and I never gave up despite any setback. Besides, I couldn't give up. I had too much to prove; especially to those few teachers who said I wouldn't amount to much. Funny how that kind of negativity can become your own personal, battle cry.

I've had several turning points but none better than the ones with my best friend and wife, Christina. We were grade school sweethearts. After 8th grade, she moved with her family to Atlanta. I promised her we'd marry someday. Of course, our lives took separate directions and we lost touch - until we reconnected in 2007 through social media. And it wasn't even Facebook - it was MySpace! Just three years later I was able to keep my 8th grade promise and we married in Hilton Head, SC.

Fast-forward 20 months from then, and we had our first miracle - Riley. We have been blessed, and I know I have been especially blessed. There's nothing more wonderful than being lucky enough to have a healthy child. Of course, Riley started a new chapter for Christina and me, but it also gave me a new purpose and mission in life - #TheLifeOfRiley.

Shortly after Riley was born, I started looking back at what I had done and what I still wanted to accomplish. Time became much more precious. I wanted to spend as much time home with Christina and Riley as I possibly could. I didn't want to miss a thing. That's when I started to "clean house" so that I wasn't wasting time on unproductive things. That meant letting some things go, which didn't end up being a big deal. When you really put things under a microscope, it's fairly easy to see what's there - or isn't there.

It also meant I had to start making good on some of the ideas I had brewing in my head for a long time. As the founder of *Networking In Atlanta*, I built a monthly event that blossomed into a monthly extravaganza with hundreds of people attending every month. For over five years, I witnessed first-hand how hundreds of people network. It was from these experiences, as well as my own networking style, that the idea for this book was first born.

My many supporters kept telling me that they've never seen anyone network like I do. And they'd never seen anyone hold anything like my monthly *Networking In Atlanta* events, which were always filled with business and sports celebrities, along with hundreds of business people. This was not just by chance of simple luck I had to earn every bit of praise. When I first moved to Atlanta, I literally went to 2-3 networking events each night. Sometimes I'd even go to 5 or 6. I personally handed out over a thousand business cards in my first month in Atlanta, and I met with serious and successful business people, politicians and celebrities every day. If you think I'm exaggerating, jump to Chapter 3: Not All Networking Is The Same.

So, that's the spirit behind this book. The passion, drive, energy and enthusiasm - along with a few tricks along the way - that I want to pass on to others so their networking becomes more than a "gotta' do activity" and really becomes a lifestyle that's fun and rewarding.

We all know there are only a few people in each field that reach the pinnacle of their field - whether sports, entertainment, business or any industry for that matter. Yes, some of them reach that height with hard work and determination plus some good old-fashioned luck. Some get driven by adversity in their lives and are on over-drive to beat that adversity. Some may even bend the rules or laws a bit to get that boost they need to succeed.

One thing is the same in everyone who reaches the pinnacle. You have to embrace every possible tool and every possible slice of energy, and you have to do it 24x7x365. My colleagues, friends, family and supporters saw me do just that in Networking. And they call it *Networking on Über Steroids*.

CHAPTER **ONE**
THE SAD STATE OF NETWORKING TODAY

Every night in every city around the world, groups hold so called networking events.

Eager business people gather together at these events to expand their base of opportunity and market knowledge. Business cards are exchanged. Sales presentations are pitched. Resumes are submitted. Prospects are identified. Follow-up meetings are scheduled. New friends are made. Sometimes even dates or hook-ups are arranged. All in hopes of meeting others who can somehow, someway help you on your path to new sales or a new job. Or whatever it is you want.

Then there are the countless books on networking. Countless is nearly thirty thousand networking books on Amazon when I last looked. Academic strategies are outlined. Tips to improve your networking are listed with a religious fervor. The good, bad and ugly of networking is discussed, shared, explored, reviewed and critiqued.

Blah, Blah, Blah.

In complete disclosure, I've only read a few networking books. Why? They all sounded alike. They all had an over-arching academic tone. They all had the same slant on networking just in slightly different words. They all bored me to death. Not a single networking book gave me an edge on how to network in today's world. I didn't learn a thing about how to "work a crowd." None of the books taught me how to pick which networking events would work best for me. And none of these books showed me how to make myself stand out at a networking event. Instead, all I got was a laundry list of items and real basic stuff.

The truth of the matter is that networking works for very few people. You probably feel the same way or you've heard others say that networking is a waste of time. The same is heard about trade shows, which are a form of networking. Most exhibitors and attendees dread going to them - except maybe for the after parties that usually accompany any good trade show. Ask anyone to show you their ROI, and you'll get a blank stare and mostly negative comments.

It's really a sad state for networking today. There's no simple answer here.

In some ways networking is the oldest form of prospecting. Way before lists of prospect leads were available for sale, networking was a sure way to meet and find new prospects. But something happened along the way.

First of all, networking events mushroomed and they became watered down. Simply put, too many events and too few quality people at the events. On top of that, the digital age affected all of us. In other words, it was a big change from the way networking was done traditionally. It's really no different than what's happened in every part of life and especially business life. The days of sending in a standard job resume and expecting a response have changed forever. Now job seekers have to resort to creative ways to get attention and get noticed.

Layer social media on top of that and you have a

real game changer. That's why I have a real problem with the way the Merriam-Webster dictionary defines networking:

"the exchange of information or services among individuals, groups, or institutions; specifically: the cultivation of productive relationships for employment or business."

Well, that's not how I define networking.

Networking is an unparalleled opportunity to create your own global community of supporters and friends that can help you and your brand advance quickly in both your professional and personal life. The keys here are: community, global and brand. You see, too many people try to network with others who have a similar interest or purpose. Too many are still thinking small or just can't see outside their own geographic space. Far too many try to do all of that without their own brand.

But let's start with what really puts networking in its sad state today. A lot has been written about how to follow-up and get results from networking events. In fact, most experts focus entirely on follow-up as the main driver to get networking results. I think it's less about follow-up and more about what you do 24x7x365. Very few live and breathe networking 24x7x365. Very few have networking in their DNA. Very few mainline steroids to get the greatest networking high they've ever experienced.

Today most see networking as a singular event or a series of events. Maybe once a month or once a week. Like minded individuals go to an event infrequently to meet like minded people with the same goals. That's why networking is in such a sad state today. It's not simply a once a month, once a week activity, hardly anyone sees networking as a 24x7x365 practice. Actually, it's not a practice. It's a lifestyle.

Now let's take a look at community. Stop think-ing that networking has to be among individuals with a common interest or goal. That's a trap that will box you in a very confined space. You'll be with others who are probably like you and want exactly what you want.

And don't fool yourself by thinking the parking garage attendant can't be in your community. How about the valet or bellman at a five-star ho-tel? How about all the execs and celebs that valet meets in a given day? The same is true of the person who shines your shoes or details your car. If you don't network with each and every person you interact with during each and every day, you and your networking are in a sad state today.

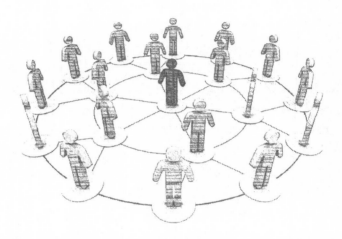

Do the math - It's been said that the average person knows at least 250 people. Then, each of these 250 people also knows another 250 people. That gives you access to 62,500 people.

Ever hear about the six degrees of separation? Before you know it, the valet who parked your car has told someone about you and that person knows someone who knows you. That creates a new opportunity.

NETWORKING ON ÜBER STEROIDS

So stop thinking networking group and *start* thinking community.

Ask yourself if you want to be a part of a community or do you want to be the community. Traditional networking will have you be a part of a group. What you really want is emotional followers who will spread the word about you and your brand. The more a community exchanges ideas around you and your brand, the more emotional they grow about the ideas. They, in turn, become influencers in that community and grow more motivated to seduce more followers to you and your brand.

Another key is not to look at networking solely as a source of sales or a job. Here's where I agree with others who say it's all about building relationships. And don't place timelines on your results. Too many people set high expectations that are unrealistic expectations. Then they stop networking because they didn't meet that ridiculous goal. It's not about winning today or tomorrow. It's all about creating the landscape that enables you to win 24x7x365.

Whatever you do, make sure to make it's global. Don't get trapped by where you live. Who says a networking event has to be limited by geography in today's world? Ever hear of Skype? Just like retail stores have found the world is their customer base, your networking opportunity is the world. We live in a global marketplace, so it is imperative to network on a global scale.

Finally, it's about your brand, your brand and your brand. Think of your brand like a sports team. Sports have fans. Fan is short for fanatic. True fanatics are guided by emotion. The key is to create physical and virtual moments for fans to share their urgency and reward them with experiences they can't find anywhere else. Your brand needs to create exclusive experiences that reward the effort of either waiting in line, being in the right place at the right time, or spending money. These moments, which hopefully will be captured by fans on social media, will help recruit others.

Every successful brand needs a set of principles that its fans can hang on to and rally others around. You need to acknowledge the love they show you, and return it. Brands doing it right regard their community members more as fans rather than customers. If you can fuel their addiction to your brand, you'll likely convert them to your cause.

Now that's my idea of networking and that's a winning step to a winning networking world. It's a blessing. And it's a curse. Just to be clear, networking is a good thing. I just don't think most people know how to really network. And I don't think most organizers know how to hold a networking event.

That's why networking is more than just a buzzword. It's probably the best opportunity you will ever have to make connections, build relationships and build your brand. And you - but only you - can make sure your networking is not in a sad state.

CHAPTER **TWO**

THE FUTURE OF NETWORKING IS ALREADY HISTORY

There has been a fundamental shift in many aspects of networking over the past decade - especially in just the last few years.

Some would say that big shifts don't come very often. They talk about cyclical patterns and a lot of other garbage. One thing should be clear. This is the digital age and past adoption rates no longer rule.

There are plenty of networking events still doing the same old, same old. Handshakes and business cards are exchanged. People walking around in an attempt to meet a few potential influencers. In all honesty, that still works for some folks. Let's say 5% to be generous. Or maybe we should just keep it more realistic and say 1%. I'm not sure about you, but those are not percentages that get me excited.

Then there are the newer events, where digital devices have been introduced to provide more functionality and productivity for the people networking at these events. Some events create a virtual directory of attendees and their presentations. You can download presentations and even the email/contact directory a few hours after the event. Soon enough, you start your own email or social media campaign as a follow-up to the networking event.

Let's also face it. Social media sites such as Twitter, Facebook and LinkedIn have created new opportunities to connect in ways we never imagined - especially for networking. But much like email and texting has caused less personal voice communications among people, social media sites have also created a dramatic shift from personal contact and relationships to keyboard communications.

That's bad news for networking *and* that's good news for networking.

It's bad if you've shifted your entire networking focus and expect email and social media to become an all or nothing solution to build your networking activities. That's the fall-out that has happened to many as a result of newer technologies and social media. To some extent, people have gotten lazy and expect that digital will be their all-encompassing answer to networking for them. It won't and it never will.

The near future (now) of networking

Now, for the good news in networking. Allow yourself to recognize the power of a totally integrated approach that includes the new, the old and leverages networking creativity - or as I would say, *Networking On ÜBER Steroids.*

So where are we now? Email and text follow-ups. Blah! Social media follow-ups. Not so blah.

There is, however, a seismic shift on its way, and it will hit networking like a ton of bricks. The near future of networking is all about 1:1 video messages integrated with social media and Skype or Facetime plus YouTube. Not blah at all.

But here's where it also gets fuzzy and ugly, and that's why I say the future is already history.

Where is networking really going to be ten years from now? Or maybe even five years from now? Not at a local venue. Trust me, it won't be the same old networking we all know. Big brands disappear. So many once-powerful brands are now just memories. And so do digital tools that become obsolete with new technologies. Skype and Facetime will soon be displaced with newer, more robust and interactive forms of meeting people anywhere, anytime in ways we never dreamed about.

First, think global. Do you have a problem dealing with people all over the world? Do you have a problem selling in Dubai? Or working there for big bucks? Just think of what has happened in retail storefronts. They've been largely displaced by e-commerce. My sister has built over 15K Instagram followers, and her US-based Shop Kouture had more customers in Australia than in most US States.

Most people still don't get this. Networking is not about your local area, unless for some reason you really want to be left behind. Take that route and I promise you one thing: there will be fewer and fewer networking opportunities and at some point you will get zero results from all the networking - if you can even find one worthwhile networking event.

Then think Google glasses. Thinking virtual networking. Think 3D. Think of walking virtually into a room with hundreds of others - maybe even thousands. Think of walking into that room in Berlin, Paris or even a city in China.

So, why is networking with digital follow-up and social media already history? Because there are businesses today, right now, already doing virtual networking. It is not a dream. It is a reality.

Networking as we know it - or as we think it will be in the next couple years - is already witnessing a revolution in digital and interactive technologies. This revolution is affecting every area of networking. Networking will become one international community linked by digital technology and the Internet. Networking will not just be a place. It will be a journey - both live and virtual - connecting thousands of people simultaneously worldwide. It means you can network anywhere. All around the world at the same time. Or different times. Or anytime you want. On demand.

Yes, these are big bold steps. I am not talking about what will happen tomorrow. It is happening today.

The opportunity for networking is tremendous. The opportunity to harness digital technology. The opportunity to transform the flow of networking and make it available to anyone, anywhere, anytime with simplicity, connectivity and speed that prior to today we only dreamed about.

We live in a dynamic new world. Business has been globalized. Competition is global. Opportunity is global. Why is networking not global then? Networking must be ubiquitous - anytime you want to network, anywhere you want to network.

I think we're all familiar with the phrase, "those

who don't learn from past mistakes are doomed to repeat them." I'd update that to "people and companies who network that don't anticipate the future of networking may not have one."

That's why networking has grown from being a business strategy to becoming a business necessity that can provide world-changing opportunities and competitive advantage beyond the digital age.

CHAPTER **THREE**

NOT ALL NETWORKING IS THE SAME

Not all networking events are the same and not all networking is the same.

Knowing which events to attend is just as important as knowing how to network at the actual event. Knowing when to bail from an event is also just as important. No matter how good you are, at some point you'll be at an event that has all pain and no gain. It happens. Even the best of networking events eventually have a loser. Could be the weather. Could be conflicting schedules. Could be whatever. When you do find yourself at a dud, run as fast as you can. Don't waste the evening - go to a different event. I've done it myself and found that the next event had all the people I thought would be at the first event.

So how do you know which events to attend?

Read the books and they'll tell you all about industries and vertical markets, common interests and goals, etc. Of course, it really depends on what your purpose is in the first place.

There are lots of books on this. Read them.

One of the most common networking groups around the country is the Young Professionals Networking. They all have a similar mission: "This group is a great way to meet interesting new people, advance your career, and give back to the community and your peers." And by the way, you don't have to be young to be at a Young Professionals event. From what I've seen, you don't even have to be professional.

There are plenty of other events driven by local organizations - from the Chamber to places of worship. These are generally a mix of people from a wide variety of backgrounds and industries. There's no rule of thumb on which one to attend. So get to all of them but don't go back unless you see, feel and touch opportunity at your first event. There are simply too many other events around so you can't waste any time on going someplace where the ROI is zero, or close to it.

There are also plenty of events driven by specific industries or professions. Again, this is part of the mix but don't rely solely on your industry or profession. Make sure you attend events in industries and for professionals not in your specific field. Remember my earlier note of caution. Whenever people at an event come from a similar background or profession, everyone is looking to score for the same reasons. Become an expert at learning about some other industries. How can your background be applied? The fact that you have experience in another field should be touted and leveraged. Your experience in another area is a plus because you bring a different point-of-view.

Bottom-line, you always want to meet quality and influential people who can help you advance quickly. No one industry or profession has a stronghold on brains. You'll find smart people and dumb people all over. So go find as many smart people as you can in as many industries as you can.

So what's really the biggest mistake people make when networking? First, I see it as thinking that all networking is event driven. It does not have to be a specific event or place. It doesn't have to be with a group with common thoughts and goals.

Here's what I'd say are some of my best networking venues:

HOTELS
Some of my best networking results have been at a couple of high-end hotels in Buckhead, an affluent area in uptown Atlanta, Georgia. (Buckhead is a major commercial and financial center of the Southeast.) When I walk in, I see hundreds of opportunities to meet people who need what I have to offer and who would like to buy what I sell. What I like most about a hotel is the fact that most of the people are likely from out-of-

town. Now you're probably wondering the six-million-dollar question: how do you meet hotel guests? I could be a smart-ass and say "network." And that would be exactly what you should do. But let me explain. Every hotel employee comes into contact with the guests. There's no one more important than the concierge followed by the bellman or bell-lady. The car valet is one of my favorites too. Make them your friends. Friends become influencers and they will reward friends. If you need more than that, the answers are later in this chapter.

RESTAURANTS

Again, all the "movers and shakers" who work at restaurants are potential influencers for you. Now it is more difficult to introduce yourself while someone is having a nice dinner. Intrude upon a romantic dinner and you can kiss your networking opportunity DOA. It's always safe to send a comp drink to that special someone you'd like to meet. But be classy about it. Thank them for producing a movie or writing a book that you found helpful - or perhaps that changed your life. Make sure your friend - the waiter or bartender or even hostess (or host) - has your business card or can tell them something short and positive about you. And never be shy about timing your bathroom urge to co-incide seconds after that person you want to meet walks to the restroom. But always, always be classy about it. And always bail if it just doesn't feel right. Never ever get close to any-thing that's like stalking or just being a pest. This is not paparazzi style of networking!

AIRPORTS

I'm fairly certain I could run a very successful sales office at any airport in the world. And I know I could stage networking events at those very same airports. What I see at every airport is opportunity. To meet, greet, befriend, persuade and network. Travelers from all walks of life and all places on the planet. It doesn't get any bet-ter than this. Sure, they're all in a hurry to get to the gate or the exit. That still leaves thousands every day at every airport who are prisoners of that airport. Some may want their peace and quiet. But give anyone something important enough to listen to - and they will listen. Thanks Delta for crating the "Delta Sky Club" where I have generated more business than anywhere else.

PLANES

If you want to find a place better than an airport,

then board the plane. I admit this can be the luck of the draw. You never know who will be sitting around you. But I see it as at least 11 people around you plus crew members, plus the rest of the passengers when boarding and de-planing. Back to those 11 people. Let's say you are in a dud situation. Maximize your odds by getting reseated. Either way, you have a lot of people in a confined space. Look at this as the best time and place to network.

CAR DEALERSHIPS

This is one of my favorites and probably also one of the easiest places to network. It's never hard to ask a guy (or gal) about their experiences with their car. Have they driven the brand? What's their experience been with the dealer-ship. Why are they there for service? I've never had a hard time getting people to talk at a dealership. And chances are your car salesper-son has a rolodex you'd like to take for a test drive yourself.

ANY CUSTOMER SERVICE LINE

Why spend time in line bitching or listening to the other people bitch? It always made more sense to me to use that time productively. It doesn't matter whether you are at a grocery store or at the airlines' counter. People are waiting impatiently and frustrated for the most part. Look at it any way you want. Help people ease their frustration level. Share common gripes to ease the pain. But do network your way to the head of the line. And then all the way to the back of the line as you leave.

ANYPLACE. ANYTIME.

Need I say more? It's not a venue. *It's everywhere.* Just network everyplace, every time, all the time. Now for the really fun stuff and why not all networking is the same...

Ask yourself the hard questions. Test yourself on how well you really do network. For starters, if you go into a networking event, do you proactively meet people. Do you aggressively do whatever is necessary to get to the front of the line? One thing is for sure; the crowd is always where the action is. Everyone wants to meet a winner. And most events don't have too many winners. So it's not always easy to get to that person. Networking isn't for the shy of heart. You should have a purpose. And you should never move on or leave because the line is too long. Never give up. Never say you'll go back when the crowd thins out. Stay the course. Go for the long haul and don't settle for anything less.

I love to people watch. At airports. Malls. The grocery store. And, of course, at networking events. I see most people walking around, looking around. Some look like they are star gazing. Others look like their eyes are star glazed. Too many won't even say hello when they're walking by you, even if you stare right at them. By the way, that's a huge problem I see in everyday life. The lack of hello or a simple "how are you" greeting is sad, very sad. Maybe you should stop wasting your time networking.

Now boarding 6 networking opportunities

And everyone - everyone - is a potential force in your networking efforts. The guy who shines

NETWORKING ON ÜBER STEROIDS

your shoes. The valet who parks your car. The maid who cleans your room. These people are real human beings. You never really know who they are. How about the shoe shiner who left thousands for his charity of choice? Meet them. Greet them. Network them.

Networking is also not a one or two-hour gig. Right now, we're at just the upfront part of net-working. Meet and greet stuff. That alone re-quires hours and hours each day. It has to be-come ingrained in your DNA. You have to do it because you like it and because you want to.

Networking really is a state of mind. If you're not up to it - stop wasting your time "trying" to network. It ain't gonna' work. Never. But if you can make the leap - getting pumped up - to a new level of energy and enthusiasm to network, join me on the journey to network on über ster-oids.

CHAPTER **FOUR**

BUILD YOUR BRAND TO BUILD YOUR NETWORKING ADVANTAGE

Over 30,000 books on networking.
Over 1,300,000 books on brands and branding.

Let me sum up all those one million plus books with one short McGraw-Hill ad that was created a few decades ago:

> *I don't know who you are*
> *I don't know your company*
> *I don't know your company's products*
> *I don't know what your company stands for*
> *I don't know your company's customers*
> *I don't know your company's reputation*
> *Now, what was it you wanted to sell me?*

*"I don't know who you are.
I don't know your company.
I don't know your company's product.
I don't know what your company stands for.
I don't know your company's customers.
I don't know your company's record.
I don't know your company's reputation.
Now—what was it you wanted to sell me?"*

MORAL: Sales start before your salesman calls—with business publication advertising.

That ad was written in the 60s. It's probably the first ad that perfectly captured the essence of branding. It was true then. And it is true now. The same can be said of almost everyone who tries to network. You, personally. And your company and its products or services.

Let's face it. Today more than ever, time is money. The proliferation of media and ads has

NETWORKING ON ÜBER STEROIDS

caused what ad people refer to as bombard-
ment. You've seen this number before: an average American consumer today is exposed to —
or "bombarded by", or "inundated with" —
5,000 advertising messages a day.

No one really knows what the real number is today. But we all know it's a big number. The
same is true of any event. And it's especially
true of individuals at these events. That's why
more than ever, you need a brand well before
you ever even begin to think about networking.
And don't make the mother of all mistakes: un-
prepared networking only to get poor, if any,
results.

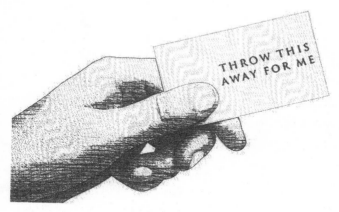

It's really better **not** to network until
you have completed your brand.

NETWORKING ON ÜBER STEROIDS

Remember, it's at least twice as hard to get someone to take a look at you the second time around. By then they already have a preconceived notion of you. Sure you can tell them you have something new to show them or talk about. Most don't give you that second chance. Even if you do get a second chance, your potential success will be negatively affected by their earlier perceptions. For some reason this whole concept is hard to accept by business people as well as job candidates. Ask yourself if a surgeon gets to operate on someone before they're ready. Ask yourself if a company rolls out a product before it's properly packaged. Yes, some do and the results are usually a disaster.

Take your time and do it right or don't do it all. There are no silver or bronze medals in networking. There's only the gold. And there's no second chances. You have one and only one chance to make an impression. Networking is not a training ground.

Start with the basics. Get a domain with your name. If your exact name is already taken, be creative and find something that is even more compelling. Nothing says you can't have fun with it. Hire someone to design a logo - keep it basic and simple with colors that match your personality and will work well across all media forms. Write up some basics about yourself and what you're all about. Launch a basic website with all of this and support it with social media.

Now that does sound a lot easier than it really is. Developing a brand is not a five-hour or even a five-day project. You have to get it right. It's probably more like five weeks. And you need to have professionals help you. Listen to those who can look at you with an objective set of eyes. Direct them but don't micro-manage them. Let their creative juices flow to create your most important and powerful asset - your brand.

Perhaps the most important element of a brand is its positioning. Go back to that McGraw-Hill ad and make sure you've answered those questions in your brand essence.

Articulate and describe who you are and what you have to offer. What edge do you offer to potential clients or employers? At the end of the day, the brand identity and its positioning should be a show-stopper and give people a reason to want to meet you, buy and possibly hire you.

A good example of positioning can be found in financial planners or wealth management advisors. You'll see words and phrases that define and articulate their brand positioning: character, competence, service. Very quickly, any prospect gets a good idea of whom they may be dealing with.

One of the most interesting industries where the personal brand has actually trumped the company brand is real estate. Just about every realtor is a member of a real estate firm and most firms are franchises. You know the brands from ReMax to Keller Williams. You'll find them almost everywhere you go. And most have dozens and dozens of agents at each location.

Now, if you are one of those realtors, you can just wait in line and get the next prospect that calls or comes in to the office.

Or maybe you already do a lot of your own marketing and get leads from that. Chances are that if you are doing that kinds of marketing, you have already branded yourself to stand apart from all the other agents in that office - and in that geographic area. It makes sense. Common sense. It's logical and fairly straightforward. All realtors can handle a transaction otherwise they wouldn't have a license. At least, we hope that's the case. The bottom-line is that realtors who brand themselves win out in every aspect of real estate sales from listings to closed transactions. There's no gray area here - except for how well you actually brand yourself.

Once you get the brand developed, you're actually back to some basics of selling. You need to make sure you are remembered. You can leave behind the same old, same old business card that usually gets thrown into a pile with hundreds of other business cards. Or you can develop special marketing tools that will help to position your brand in a very memorable way.

My business card for over ten years was a poker chip with BetONBrandON.com and nothing else! The Poker Chip itself is made of the same material you will find at The Bellagio in Las Vegas. Trust me, they get noticed. They get remembered.

Another friend hands out large and heavy coins as his business cards. Again, a very impressive and memorable way to get noticed. There's no magic here, and I would argue that branding isn't all that new anyway. Passing out a unique business card isn't a fully developed brand by any means, but it is a basic ABC of branding. If you can't afford to complete an entire branding effort, do at least this one thing right. Create a brand business card that is powerful and compelling. It may be your only tool, but it can be one hell of a tool.

Of course, branding is also a lot more than a clever logo and memorable business leave-behinds. Your brand needs to be infused in everything you do. And I mean everything. What clothes you wear. Your car. The restaurants you pick. Yes, even your smell can be part of your brand. Did you ever notice that certain stores have a very distinct aroma? It's probably not by accident.

The proliferation of your brand into everything you do is what makes your brand identity compelling and memorable. Make sure each and every social media you launch has the brand all over it. And make sure you even get some of those crazy but useful "tchotchkes" (giveaways) to always leave behind. But just like I illustrated with business cards, don't get junk. Make sure

your giveaways are clever, have the brand plas-
tered on it - and have some connection to you
and your brand. (Yes, I have what looks like a
steroid needle but is actually a flash drive with
this book on it.)

I should also point out that this book is not intended to be Branding On Über Steroids. (That
one is in the works already.) But ramp up your
networking with some of the basics I've described today, and your Networking will begin
to feel like it's on steroids.

NETWORKING ON ÜBER STEROIDS

CHAPTER **FIVE**

INVENTING YOUR NETWORKING STRATEGY FOR THE SOCIAL AGE

Assuming you have properly branded yourself and your services, you are now ready for the social age where that brand can be launched and reinforced every minute of every day, all around the world. Make sure you are visible on every possible social media platform.

However, don't over extend yourself by registering on everything and then failing to keep up with each social media site. There's nothing worse than being on something - but not really. What does it say about you if you haven't posted anything recently? In today's world if you don't post daily, you become irrelevant. That's no way to build a brand and build your networking.

If you simply don't have time to manage a lot of

social media platforms, then prioritize. Pick the top 3 or 4 that you can keep updated periodically throughout the day. A lot of tools out there can help you publish on multiple social media platforms. Use them. Which social media sites you select is based on what it is you are trying to accomplish and who you are targeting. Facebook, Twitter and LinkedIn frequently become the first 3 standards for a lot of people. Whether you select Instagram or Snapchat may depend on your brand. Others like Foursquare have a different purpose but can also be a part of the mix.

It's not the social network you choose; it's how you use it.

How you use social media for networking becomes the core of your networking strategy. This is also where most people tend to be timid and rarely ever proactive. Posting things about yourself can be cute. It may be informative for family and friends. But if you are using social media to network, you need a different game plan. You need to target and you need to do some homework to target. You need to set specific goals. What do you want to get out of that post?

Let me share an example that goes beyond networking. A lot of road warriors and frequent flyers have become dismayed with frequent guest programs. That's easy to understand. Most programs are based on satisfying a large group of customers and that group is usually segmented by their activity of buying from a specific business. Recently, there have been a lot of reductions in those programs. That has caused a lot of disgruntled customers. You don't need to be disgruntled. Social media posts are the best way to get additional acknowledgements from a brand. Businesses understand the power of posts - both positive and negative. Get yourself rewarded and get yourself out of the pack mentality - post about your experiences.

The posts must be targeted to support and reinforce your brand. The posts must be targeted to touch the hot buttons of your targets. The posts must be customized to the point of being one-on-one. Always remember to add your targets to your posts otherwise they won't even know what you've posted. I see far too many posts, especially on Instagram and Twitter, that don't add the name of the entitiy they are talking about. Don't be shy. Use hashtags. Use everything possible to make sure your posts are working for you and they are networking for you.

Now, for the action from social media and networking events, networking places and virtual networking. If you've done all the right things up front - from branding and social media to a steroid attitude with a non-stop work ethic, results will happen. It may sound silly but how you manage those results will spell success or failure. Not being ready for the action is not an unusual mistake - it's common across all fields and all industries. Some statistics prove that 77% of sales leads go unanswered. Whatever the number may be, even one sale lead that goes unanswered is unacceptable. So how you handle all the action from your networking activity?

Now for some of the basics of networking - not just for the social age but for all ages. Some of these may be obvious but they are always worth reinforcing.

Always first, you don't have time to waste and you need to believe that with absolute certainty. Let every prospective customer know through your actions and words, because there are plenty of people willing to waste your time. Not to say you should be rude. *There are plenty of ways to convey this in a polite, even friendly way.*

Bottom line, you are in business to make money! If networking is not making you money, you're wasting your time. If you're not doing it right, you're wasting your time. People who are serious about making money *don't waste time...*

3 GROUND RULES FOR *"DOING IT RIGHT"*

1. Be Authentic

You are the only person who can authentically be you. That's what makes you unique. That's your advantage. You know that you are being yourself when you're the same person no matter where you are or who you are with. Be authentic – nobody wants to do business with a phony. People buy from people they like and trust.

2. Be Open 24/7/365

We've all heard that people come into our life for a reason. That's not just the people you meet at networking meetings. In fact, most of them come in to waste your time or we could say to teach you how to protect your time.

Any one you meet has the potential to bring lucrative opportunities to you; from your friend, the financial genius, to the guy who stacks the carts at Publix, a regional grocery store.

For all you know, that guy is brilliant, connected and has life experiences he would gladly share with you if only you would consider him worth a few minutes of your time. Engage with the people you meet at Starbucks, on the plane and at the ballpark.

3. Be Quiet and Listen

People love to talk about themselves. It's the rare person that shows up to listen. Be that person. By actively listening to what the people say, you gather information, learn what's important to them and figure out just where you can (or cannot) provide value.

Besides, you'll be more memorable than the hundreds of others who talked rather than listened.

3 GROUND RULES FOR "MAKING IT PAY"

1. Know What You Sell

Whenever someone asks what you do or sell, tell them in concise and clearly defined terms. Whether you are selling a product or you are the product, make it easy for people to know what you're offering and if they want to buy.

Don't waste time selling to someone who is not buying.

2. Know Who Buys What You Sell?

Know exactly who your target market is. Although you believe that everyone can benefit from your product, you only want the people who will buy. Then, qualify your prospects quickly to determine if they will buy from you.

Remember, you don't have time to waste.

3. Know How To Close A Sale

If you can't close a sale, you have no business networking. I'm not saying you have to close sales at networking events. In fact, in most cases, that's the worst move you can make. What

I'm saying is – when the time comes to close the deal, you better know how to nail it down. If you don't, invest your time in sales training.

I know a guy who can help;
oh yeah, you already know him.

So STOP wasting time networking. If you're in the game, learn to play it well. Develop the skills you're missing and get out there and net-work. *Do it right and make it pay!*

STOP WASTING TIME *just* **NETWORKING**

CHAPTER **SIX**

IT'S ALL ABOUT EXECUTION, EXECUTION & EXECUTION

One thing is for sure. Going to one and only one event or networking function is okay for starters - But do it right all the way from the beginning to the end. There's nothing worse than a poor performance during any step of the process.

It's not too difficult to find the right event to go to. Sure you'll have a few hits and you'll have your share of misses. In the unlikely event you find every event you've attended a total bust, you probably need to dig deeper into what you are doing at the events. Or you can always just drop the idea of attending staged events and just go the distance at other forms such as the local five-star hotel or restaurants.

Most networking falls apart right up front because of a shy, timid or just lazy approach. Successful networking requires passion, drive, energy, enthusiasm, stamina and maybe even some steroids. Let's face the facts. Networking is no different than any other field. Only the top 1% of networkers are at the top of the networking game. If you want to make the major leagues in networking, same-old, same-old won't cut it.

Even with all the greatest branding in the world, your networking efforts will fall apart if you aren't guided by execution, execution and execution. So what do I mean by the triple-play execution? Create an attitude with relentless determination and steroid power that gets you to the pinnacle each and every time. Nothing less will do. Nothing less wins.

It's all about EXECUTION!

It's a big world out there and there are others who play major leagues too. I've always known that ever since I was a young kid. I have always wanted to be the best at what I do. I may not have achieved the elusive top spot every time, but I did attempt to hit it every time. It's my over-eagerness to compete, win and standout. Clenched teeth, white knuckles and desire – I have always been determined to make something happen. I always see the prize in my mind. At the end of the day, I can boil it down to just a few power traits. Call it Networking On über Steroids if you'd like. But always call it Networking like you've never seen before.

BRASS BALLS

You know what I mean and no offense intended for any gender. Cut the shy crap. You want to meet someone who could make a difference in your life? Trust me. They are not waiting around for you and they aren't looking for you. Make yourself visible. Be creative and work the people and system that surround your networking opportunity. I didn't get to meet Lil' Wayne by waiting in line. I created a new line to him and I was at the head of that line. I didn't get on Bieber's bus because they picked me out of a line. I worked his bus people until I was one of the bus people.

LASER VISION

Whenever you want to meet that special some-one, make sure you get a laser focus on your target. You can't be sidetracked by all the noise around you. And you can't reach your target if you don't see it clearly. If you're looking around to see what other networking opportunities may be present, your vision on your initial target is already blurred. If you're not consistently and persistently seeing the target, move to the right place until you do. If you want to hit the bull's eye, set your laser vision to that - and only that bull's eye.

RUTHLESS & DEMANDING

There's that old saying "those who shout the loudest get heard the most." Well it's definitely not the shouting that works in networking. That's how you annoy others - not network. I prefer to be very persistent almost to the point of being ruthless. I prefer to be demanding al-most to the point of being obnoxious. Never cross the line on those points. But never be soft either because only the ruthless and demanding network on steroids.

ON DEMAND

You need to drop everything and everyone whenever an opportunity arises. Opportunities are time sensitive. Here today, gone tomorrow is actually here right now, gone in a second. It's true of every part in the networking process. From initial contact to follow-up, you have to make it on demand. Don't wait to email a follow-up. Do it right then, right there. You'll have a better chance of meeting that person again at that time, at that place rather than the next day somewhere else.

PERSISTENT PATIENCE

I guess it's kind of like a stake-out. You wait and wait. You keep your eye on the target. You make your move when it's all clear. But in between all of that, time is filled with persistent patience. Occasionally you get lucky and get to network with your #1 opportunity quickly. But that rarely happens. Networking isn't about this week, this month or even this year. Want to network with the White House staff? Have persistent patience that can endure an entire administration's stay there. Yes, sometimes it takes years.

PERSISTENT FOLLOW UP

Right now, take a look at how you handle follow-ups. After connecting with someone, do you wait a day or two? Maybe longer? How about once you do the first follow-up? Do you give up if you haven't heard anything the second time around? How about the third time? Or fourth time? What's your bottom-line? My father once put a sales candidate through dozens and dozens of interviews and meetings. They didn't happen over days. They didn't happen over months. He knew he had the right candidate because she would have followed-up for years if that's what it took. Networking is no different.

Rock solid networking takes all that and more. It's that relentless pursuit with an almost super-human level of energy that gives you Networking On Über Steroids for a lifetime.

CHAPTER **SEVEN**
CREATE YOUR NETWORKING CONTENT

*Most great PR experts, as well as most success-
ful business people and especially salespeople,
can shout out an elevator pitch in under 30
seconds.*

If you're not familiar with the term "elevator
pitch," it's simply a brief but succinct description
of what you are offering and its value proposi-
tion. Let's assume you know what you want to
say. In all likelihood, it would take you 4-5
minutes to get through all those wonderful
things you'd like someone to hear. No one will
listen that long - certainly not the first time when
you are networking.

You need to grab someone's attention quickly
and give them as much information as possible.
It has to be the most important and relevant information that touches their "hot buttons" or

points of interest. Say the wrong things and you've lost that opportunity. Say the right things and take five minutes and you've lost that opportunity. Why? They stop listening after thirty seconds.

Think of great advertising. Why are billboards eye-catching, short and right to the point? Why are broadcast ads 60 seconds or less? Attention spans are getting shorter and shorter. Media is bombarding everyone every second of the day. It's made us a nation of media clutter. It's made us a nation of sound bites. When you are ready to network and deliver that all-important sound bite, you have to stop the traffic all around you so that person focuses on you. You can't do that if you ramble.

Everyone is vying for your attention. Share it wisely.

You'll hear a lot of push back on an elevator pitch. People will say the product is too complicated to wash down in 30 seconds. Others say I need more time to adequately talk about it - no one will understand in 30 seconds.

How about no one wants to spend more than 30 seconds listening to you? Why do you think commercials tend to be 30 seconds - and now 10-15 seconds spots have become commonplace? Let's face it. It's all about time and competing messages. Whether broadcast, online or networking, you need to stop traffic. Call it a sound bite. Call it an elevator pitch. Call it whatever you want. Make it ear-catching, traffic-stopping and deliver it like you're on stage or on the court.

Just a final thought here on the initial contact, never make the golden mistake here and end by saying "you could explain more if you had more time." Because they'll remember you for that last sound bite. If you don't get the nod of approval, go back and change the pitch until you get it right. At some point, you can go back to those who didn't give you the high five and let them know exactly that. "Hey, I blew it when I first met you but I learned my lesson so here it is." Needless to say, if you're lucky enough to get a second chance, there probably won't be a third chance so get it right.

Now for the more difficult part of creating net-working content for the follow-up, follow-up and follow-up. Relevance is the key - followed by timely consistency! It always has been and always will be. Somehow, with so much content in the world in so many media forms, we all try to say so much. It's almost like a game of how much can you get out from email and text to posts. Think about it. Just a couple decades ago, it was a phone-call and mailed letter. Then it was streamlined to email. Now it's become email + text + FB post + Insta post + T post + YouTube upload +++++++.

My father told me a funny but true story of when he was the CMO of EarthWeb. The founding CEO became one of the brightest stars of the Dotcom era. He understood that timing was everything. He knew that a minute late was a lost opportunity forever. Back to the story, my Dad had offices on both the 32nd and 36th floors of the building EarthWeb occupied on Park Avenue in NYC. He literally walked up and down those four flights every hour because NYC elevators leave a lot to be desired when you're in a rush. So whenever the EarthWeb CEO needed my Dad, he'd first call his 32nd floor desk. Knowing that my Dad might be on the 36th floor or somewhere in between, the CEO simultaneously hit every possible mode of contact: my Dad's cell phone, my Dad's pager, his 36th floor office, 36th floor receptionist, 32nd floor receptionist, his admin, his team members all while sending someone to walk the stairs up to the 36th floor. On one day, my Dad took the elevator which got stuck between the 36th and 32nd floors At least the rescue team was on its way!

So the point is that you have to be timely. Actually timely isn't enough - it has to be uber-timely. And yes, you have to hit all points of content distribution these days. Simultaneously!

Now for the relevance - almost everyone still speaks in "speeds and feeds." Networkers boast how they and their products or services can do this and do that. They talk about being #1 in their field. In the world. They talk value, ROI and TCO (total cost of ownership), lifetime values and so much more. Not that long ago, most people figured out that speeds and feeds were usually totally irrelevant because it was generic and didn't relate to how it would help a certain company or individual.

That's true today more than ever. If you are interviewing for a job, do you speak speeds and feeds? Do you fall into the trap of reciting a laundry list of accomplishments? Do you tell them you graduated from a certain school and got a certain award? Or do you tell them what it means to them.

Let me give you an example of how my father was able to turn his academics into a relevant dialogue. In fact, it became the major reason he was highly recruited by some of the Japanese giants such as NEC and NTT. Rather than that huge laundry list in a resume, he would tell them: his career got fast-tracked just like he got a BS degree in three years from RIT, a world-renowned college that stressed technology and business before others - and where he was selected as Distinguished Alumnus of the Year from their Saunders College of Business, which has a presence in Japan, Dubai, Italy, Turkey and 8 other countries. In the few seconds it took him for that, he connected with them on a number of relevant levels while boasting his credentials in a very humble way.

Now it does take some homework to be truly relevant. Know everything you can about the person or people you want to network with. Research their website, their collaterals, their press releases and search the web for people background information. Do one of the most basic but proven business diagrams in the world: Strengths, Weaknesses, Opportunities and Threats (SWOT). You'd be surprised how a few minutes of homework and organizing your findings will help any dialogue.

With all of that relevant research, you now have a gold mine of information that can be used to write follow-up emails, post social media posts and some good old hard fashion marketing that just might include sending some items by snail mail.

Each and every follow-up message must be rich with factoids and rich with how you can offer value. It's not enough to say you do something well. You must give specifics. At some point after you have received some networking connection, you need to step up your game and get them to become a part of your community. Let them see who you are, the company you keep, your daily wins and kudos.

None of this is rocket science. But it is a well-oiled formula that works if you are persistent and execute rapidly with relevant content. If you do that, you will be Networking on Über Steroids.

CHAPTER **EIGHT**

WHERE IN THE WORLD ARE MY STEROIDS?

We all know the pitfalls of creating super human performance with steroids.

Let me just clear the air here. I'm not a fan of that approach at all. It's not fair in sports and has brought shame to those who used them. It has also brought shame and loss of credibility to organizations and countries around the world. Then there's the whole slew of health risks to be considered.

But I am a huge fan of gaining a competitive edge to beat out the competition and out-perform the competition. Gaining that edge can be done in any sport or any field the hard, old-fashioned way. Practice, practice, practice. That's how you get to Carnegie Hall and that's how you become successful networking.

Your steroids are everywhere and nowhere. Some of us have it in our DNA. It's the way we are wired and it comes naturally. Others have to get to that state-of-mind where one can network flawlessly and enjoy the benefits of the wins along the way - and not get down when rejections appear over and over again. Still others have to do it the hard way. No matter how you get there, the results can be fantastic, rewarding and enjoyable.

The only obstacle to successful networking is you. Don't listen to the naysayers. There's always a lot of people who say it can't be done. Remember those teachers I described who told me I wouldn't be successful? There's always a lot of people who will tell you to slow down - "don't be too aggressive." Just remember you'll never be in first place by slowing down. And there's always people who will tell you to the time is not right or they're not interested.

Never say "never" to yourself. And never say "I can't" to yourself. Networking is no longer an option. It is a business reality. Just networking is no longer an option. Networking on steroids is a business necessity.

So stop wasting your time just networking. Take away some of the ideas, some of the strategies and tactics and some of the hints I've described in this book so you can start **networking on ÜBER steroids.**

NETWORKING ON ÜBER STEROIDS

ACKNOWLEDGEMENTS

This book has been a work-in-progress for many, many years. Even the idea of it started years ago. That's because I have had so many wonderful and loving people in my life that have encouraged, motivated and inspired me to reach my lofty goals. Now I have the opportunity to share my thoughts with others.

First, I am so thankful for my best friend and wife, Christina. She turned my life around. She has been my greatest cheerleader - always there, always listening and always on my side. And, of course, to both Christina and Riley. They are the reason why I get up every day and get fired up to do right. It's really very simple. I want to make them proud and I want to make sure I give back to them as much as they have given to me.

Next, I can't begin to put into words what my parents have done for me. By now you probably realize that I never got anyplace the easy way and I do test and stretch the limits in everything I do. Well, that's especially true of those turbulent teenage years. Somehow I always managed to escape any real trouble. And that's largely due to the fact that my parents never, ever gave up on me.

They've always been there. And they continue to be there. My father will drop everything to help me out whenever I need his advice. And my mother does the same thing for me and my family. Nothing like having an RN on call all the time.

NETWORKING ON ÜBER STEROIDS

By the way, I was far from being an only child. While sibling rivalry might have been a part of growing up, I admire and respect my younger brother, Ryan, and my younger sister, Kiley, for all their accomplishments. Ryan is a rock solid businessman and has risen the management ranks at Target very, very quickly. He was one who always excelled at school and sports. And he's still always the one who is always there for me and for us. His fiancé, Lamija, is an absolutely adorable person and they make a great couple. Ryan may be younger than me, but he's already showing signs of becoming the family patriarch. Kiley launched a very successful online fashion boutique called Shop Kouture at a young age. Her talents are world-class and makes a fashion statement in everything she does. What makes her a real special sister and family member is how often she has dropped everything to help out. From being with my grandmother through a very difficult end-of-life journey, to becoming a mother figure to the DeVivo sisters, we can always count on her.

And then there's the DeVivo sisters (#vivosisters), my incredible nieces, Morgan, Molly, Lily and Lucy. Whenever I think I'm overwhelmed doing stuff, I think of my brother-in-law, the super Dad, Owen. Among the DeVivo sisters, there's a set of twins and there's a whole lot of organized chaos and fun times that Owen seems to manage with ease. Morgan is the oldest and already a teenager so we've been close for many, many years. Let's say she's more like a sister to me and sometimes, even a daughter to Christina and myself. We love her dearly and know she'll only become closer to us in the next few years. A lot of people, rightfully so, say negative things about the new-age of teenagers. Morgan disproves that each and every day. She can be as old-fashioned as my grandmother - and she can be as hip as any of her classmates. Most of all, she's genuine inside and out.

When I married Christina, I became much more than just her mother and father's son-in-law. I became a part of a family – and we've all been through some rough spots as well as the joyous times. I also have a wonderful sister-in-law, Alicia, and I really enjoy my time with her husband, Sam, and their kids, Mason and Tyler. Alicia is a Vet and Sam holds more degrees than I can count. Yet, you'd never know any of that because he's a real down-to-earth kind of guy. Of course, our families had already known each other for years while Christina and I were in grade school back in Rochester. In many ways, it seems that we've all been family since I was a little kid. Let's just say it was all meant to be.

I know I'm lucky. And I know I wouldn't be here today if it wasn't for the consistent and continued love and support of my family and each and every member of my family that has been there for me - and continues to be there for me.

I also have to look back at the teachers who have impacted my life. While I mentioned a few of the "nay-sayers," it's far more important to thank those who took the extra time and effort to "teach" me. Ironically, they had to learn how to understand me first. But they took the time to do that. To appreciate me. To see my possibilities. To inspire my dreams. To build my confidence. To boost my confidence. To encourage me. I can't name all of them. But I do have a special thanks for Mrs. J and Mr. San.

Then there are the incredible mentors, friends and colleagues. I'm not sure names mean much for a book because they know who they are. But to "Pa" aka Mr. Pelusio and BT, a special thanks. Dave, Keith, Nate, Dan, Andrew, Matt, Joey, Tom, John, CB, Thomas, Rich, Adam and Hillel -

special thanks too. As you can imagine, in the past few years, some friends have become mentors, and some mentors have become friends. From former U. S. Secret Service agents to the #1 Sales Guru of the world, Jeffrey Gitomer, to super celebs like Lil Wayne and super performing business execs like Reggie Bradford - I can't thank you enough for helping get to this point.

There are many more thanks to be given. Especially to all the members of Networking In Atlanta and all the clients who have supported me through the years.

However, there is one more person I want to acknowledge. In 1924 in a small town in Germany, Elizabeth Huber was born. Her life was filled with immense hardships. Yet she overcame poverty, the death of her parents before she was six, war ravaged living conditions and even the lack of a basic education. She fought back the obstacles. She placed every ounce of energy she had to succeed despite the odds she was born into. She taught those principles to my father. And she taught those principles to me right up to her death on April 6, 2012. Christina, Riley and I were lucky enough to see her during those last days. And I was lucky enough to have her support and encouragement through every day of my life. I always wanted to make her proud of me. My father says I have.

Danke sehr, Grandma!

87582746R00052

Made in the USA
Lexington, KY
26 April 2018